Arctic CHILL!

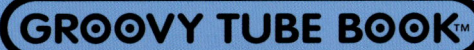

GROOVY TUBE BOOK™

written by SUSAN RING
illustrated by BERNARD ADNET

Line art by Roseanne Kakos-Main
Game by Eric Berlin

Photo page 16: Rick Stanley
Copyright © 2004 by innovative KIDS®
All rights reserved
Published by innovative KIDS®, a division of innovative USA®
18 Ann Street, Norwalk, CT 06854
Printed in China
10 9 8 7 6 5 4 3

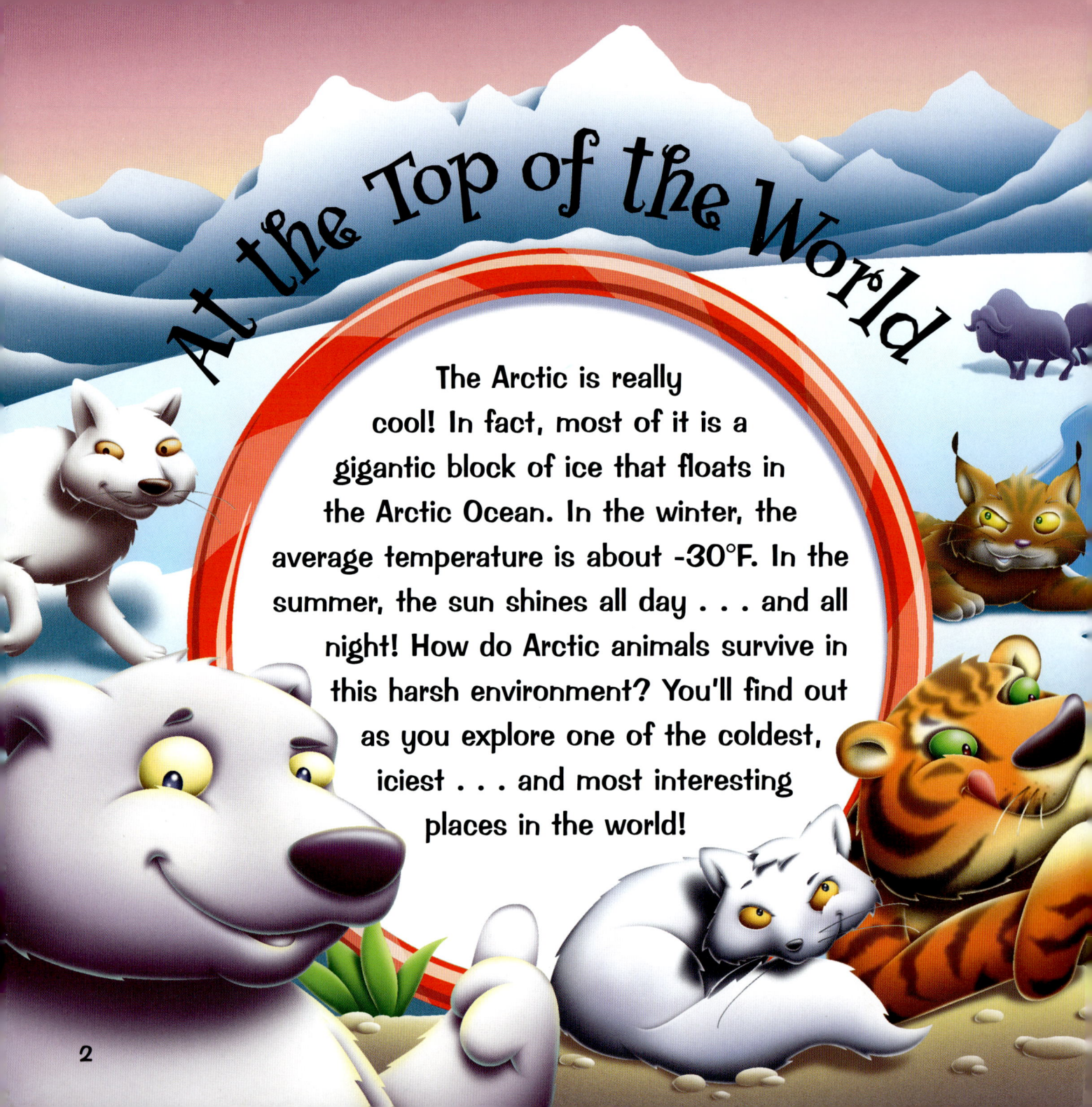

At the Top of the World

The Arctic is really cool! In fact, most of it is a gigantic block of ice that floats in the Arctic Ocean. In the winter, the average temperature is about -30°F. In the summer, the sun shines all day . . . and all night! How do Arctic animals survive in this harsh environment? You'll find out as you explore one of the coldest, iciest . . . and most interesting places in the world!

King of the Arctic

The polar bear is the biggest of all bears and the largest mammal that lives in the Arctic. This mighty bear can weigh over 1,000 pounds and is a super swimmer.

Polar bears hunt seals. A polar bear will wait next to a seal's airhole until the seal pops up from the water to breathe. Then the bear pounces! In summer, polar bears dine on seaweed, mussels, and whales that have washed up on the shore.

Female polar bears *hibernate*, or sleep for several months, during the winter. First, the female polar bear digs a big den in the snow. Before going inside, she eats lots of food to build up her fat, or *blubber*.

A polar bear
hunts for dinner.

Mother polar bears usually have two cubs at a time. They're born inside the den. The babies are born without any teeth. They can't see, hear, or walk for several weeks. They drink their mother's rich milk and grow quickly.

Polar bears wrestle in the snow.

Cold Facts

Polar bears really don't have white fur! Each hair is clear—it has no color at all. Reflecting sunlight makes it look white! The hairs stick together and make a waterproof "swimsuit" that protects the bears from the freezing waters.

The Hunters and the Hunted

Lynxes are members of the cat family. Their long legs and big feet allow them to run across deep snow without sinking.

Lynxes sneak up on their prey and quickly leap on top of them. Their favorite food is snowshoe hare, but they'll also eat birds and small deer. Sometimes lynxes will hide part of their prey to eat later.

A sneaky lynx on the prowl

Two ferocious
Arctic wolves

Arctic wolves are also fierce hunters. They are part of the gray wolf family, and they hunt together in groups called packs. A wolf pack usually has one leader and between eight to twenty other members.

Members of an Arctic wolf pack howl as a way of talking to each other. They call to each other while they hunt for musk oxen, caribou, and moose.

Despite their name, wolverines are actually related to weasels, not wolves. They eat small mammals, birds, and plants, but caribou are their favorite prey. Wolverines will chase after a caribou for miles, then jump on its back to bring it down. These vicious hunters have powerful jaws that can eat meat that is frozen solid and can even chew through bone.

Cold Facts

Wolverines are only three feet long, but they can defend themselves even against polar bears, which are up to four times as large!

Keeping Warm

How can animals survive in the freezing Arctic? Walruses have thick layers of blubber underneath their skin, but also keep warm by huddling in large groups. They have to be careful not to bump into their neighbors' sharp tusks, which can grow up to three feet long! Walruses use their tusks to haul their heavy bodies—up to 2,200 pounds— onto the ice from the water.

Big, blubbery walruses huddle together.

Musk oxen have short, extra-wide hooves that prevent them from sinking too deep in the snow. Their sharp hooves also help them to get at plants buried under the snow.

Musk oxen are not really oxen; they are part of the goat family. The long hairs on the outside of their bodies are called guard hairs. Underneath their guard hair is a layer of woolly fur. All these shaggy layers keep them warm and dry.

Musk oxen travel together in small herds of about fifteen to twenty. The adults surround the babies to keep them safe from enemies such as wolves.

A musk ox treads through deep snow.

Hiding in Plain Sight

When animals have the same color as their surroundings, it is called *camouflage*. Animals with camouflage can hide more easily. Arctic hares, Arctic foxes, and ermine have fur coats that turn white in the winter— ideal for their snowy environment. The Arctic fox can even curl its own bushy tail around itself, just like a built-in blanket!

In the summer, their coats change to brown to blend in better with the rocks and soil of the tundra.

Left: An Arctic hare, on alert for danger

Left: An Arctic fox keeps himself warm with his bushy tail.

Mommy and baby
harp seal

Newborn harp seals, called
pups, also have soft, snowy-white
fur, which helps keep them safe
on the ice. After a few weeks,
their fur turns gray and spotted—
a color that will protect them
from whales and sharks in the
icy water.

Cold Facts

The coat of a harp
seal pup is called a
"ragged jacket" when it
starts to molt. Molting is
when the white fur starts
to fall off, leaving the
adult gray fur.

It's a Long, Long Way

A caribou shows off its impressive antlers.

Caribou—also known as reindeer—live on the Arctic tundra. But before the harsh winter arrives, caribou *migrate* to the south, where the climate is warmer. Caribou have the longest migration of any land animal—a thousand miles every year.

To prepare for such a long journey, caribou spend their summers eating constantly—a caribou eats about ten pounds of food a day! Their favorite food is *lichens*, tiny plants that grow on rocks or trees in the cold Arctic.

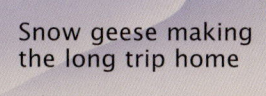

Snow geese making the long trip home

Several types of birds migrate thousands of miles each year to spend summers in the Arctic. Snow geese spend up to sixteen hours a day feeding on Arctic plants before flying south at summer's end.

The Arctic tern makes the longest migration—over 21,000 miles—from the North Pole to the South Pole and back. The female lays eggs in the Arctic in the summer months, then flies to the Antarctic for the winter.

An Arctic tern feeds its hatchling.

Cold Facts

When snow geese are migrating, they sometimes fly so high up in the air that they can barely be seen from the ground far below!

Birds of a Feather

The Arctic is home to many unusual birds. Among these are puffins—seabirds that spend most of their lives in the water. They go on land only to nest.

Puffins can stay out at sea for a long time because they can drink salt water. A special hole in their noses releases the salt they take in. These birds stay warm and waterproof in the icy waters because their feathers trap and hold warm air.

A puffin makes a rare appearance on land.

Puffins dive underwater for food and will swallow while under the water. To get airborne, puffins run across the water to pick up speed, then take off into the sky.

Also unusual is the ptarmigan, which has feathers on its feet—it can walk on top of deep snow!

The white snowy owl is found only in the Arctic. Most other types of owls are *nocturnal*, or active at night. But the snowy owl hunts during the day, making its white camouflage feathers even more impotant!

Above: A ptarmigan rests comfortably on the snow.

Cold Facts

Not all Arctic birds need white camouflage. Ravens have black feathers that absorb and hold the heat from the sun. Ravens are very clever, acrobatic birds and have been known to steal food from other animals!

Left: A snowy owl has spotted you!

Water Giants

Whales are massive sea creatures that live in Arctic waters all year long. Whales are mammals, not fish. They must come up to the surface of the water to breathe air. Like other large Arctic mammals, whales have lots of blubber to keep them warm.

One of the strangest-looking whales is the narwhal. Male narwhals have a long tusk that sticks out of their upper lip. This tusk is about three feet long, and it's actually a tooth! Some people think that the narwhal inspired the legend of the unicorn.

A narwhal swims through Arctic waters. Look out for that tooth!

Beluga whales are also called "white whales" even though they're really a gray color. These vocal whales will chirp, grunt, and even baa like a lamb.

A beluga whale surfaces for a breath of fresh air.

Cold Facts

Bowhead whales can grow to be 65 feet long and are classified as baleen whales. A baleen whale takes in water and filters out tiny plants and shrimp for its food. It's hard to believe such a huge creature can survive on such a small food source. But studies have shown that bowhead whales can live to be 100 years old!

Wide OPEN spaces

The *tundra* is the open, rocky land around the Arctic Ocean. The ground there is always frozen, but in the summer, the soil gets warm enough for small plants to grow. These are eaten by the small animals that call the tundra home.

Arctic foxes live in the tundra all year round. They are *carnivores*, which means they eat other animals, such as mice and lemmings. The foxes compete for these rodents with other carnivores such as weasels and snowy owls. Clever Arctic foxes will store their prey under the ground and eat their secret snacks when there is no other food to be found.

An Arctic fox roaming the summer tundra.

A moose with
a full-grown
rack of antlers

Moose, the largest type of deer, also live in the tundra. They reach heights of over six feet tall. And that doesn't include the males' enormous antlers, which take seven years to grow to full size. Each winter after that, moose shed their antlers and grow new sets every spring.

Cold Facts

Moose have been known to swim across rivers that are miles wide. Sometimes they'll dive under the water to grab some plants. They can eat 43 pounds of plants each day!

Into the Woods

Beyond the tundra is the *taiga*, which is cold and snowy most of the year, but warms up enough in the summer to grow trees— poplars, evergreens, and birches.

The Siberian tiger makes its home in the taiga. Also called the Amur tiger, it is the largest of all tigers. Siberian tigers change their fur color along with the seasons: Their fur is reddish gold in the summer and pale yellow in the winter.

A Siberian tiger wanders through the taiga.

Another animal found in the taiga is the prickly porcupine. Porcupines are born with 30,000 quills! They're excellent tree climbers and eat berries, nuts, tree bark, and pine needles. Baby porcupines are called porcupettes. Luckily for their mothers, porcupettes have soft quills when they are born. But the quills become stiff within a few days. When a baby porcupine gets grumpy, it throws a temper tantrum. It will swat its tail, stomp its feet, and let out a stink bomb.

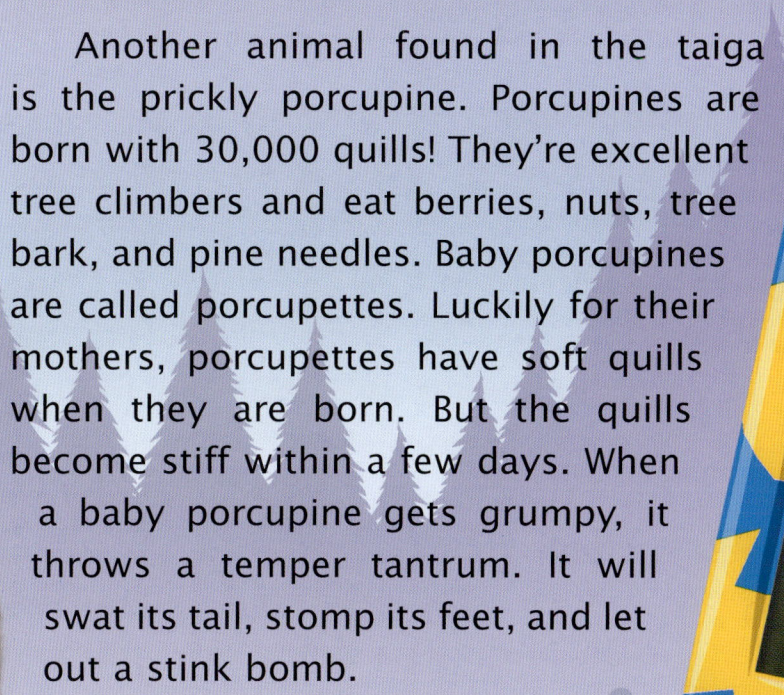

A baby porcupine has soft quills.

Cold Facts

The taiga is also home to flying squirrels. They don't really fly but glide in the air from tree to tree.

The Arctic in Danger

The Arctic is a special place. Sadly, there are many threats to this beautiful environment. An increasing number of tourists and industries in the Arctic disturb wildlife habitats. Fishing boats sometimes catch seals in their nets. Polar bears and whales are in danger of becoming extinct because of overhunting.

Pollution is also a big threat. Exhaust from cars is warming the Earth, which will drastically affect Arctic wildlife.

If we protect the land of the Arctic now, the animals will continue to live and thrive there . . . and this beautiful frozen land will be there to enjoy in the future.

Cold Facts

A laboratory in Canada called Igloolik looks like a flying saucer from outer space! Scientists there gather information about the wildlands of the Arctic, so we can learn how to protect the Arctic for the future.

23

Arctic Animal Adventure

Use these questions to play the board game!

1. What word means "to move to a warmer climate during cold weather?"

2. In the summer, the sun shines in the Arctic even at night. True or False?

3. Polar bears can't swim. True or False?

4. In what region can trees grow in the Arctic—tundra, taiga, or ice cap?

5. Why do walruses huddle in large groups?

6. Polar bear babies are born with over 100 teeth. True or False?

7. A Siberian tiger's fur changes color with the seasons. True or False?

8. Spell the word "migration."

9. Lynxes are related to which animal: Cats or dogs?

10. Moose can swim. True or False?

11. Wolverines are related to wolves. True or False?

12. An animal whose coat is the same color as its environment is said to have what?

13. What is the thick layer of fat on a walrus called?

14. What do you call the outer hairs on a musk ox?

15. What shiny black bird lives in the Arctic?

16. What name is given to a group of wolves?

17. Spell the word "caribou."

18. About two weeks after birth, a harp seal turns what color?

19. What animal acquires a "ragged jacket" as it begins to molt?

20. By what other name are caribou known?

21. The temperature in the Arctic can reach 30°F below zero. True or False?

22. Polar bear hairs are not white, but clear. True or False?

23. Newborn harp seals have black fur. True or False?

24. What land animal has the longest migration?

25. What are the tiny plants that grow on Arctic rocks and trees called?

26. The Arctic tern flies over 20,000 miles every year. True or False?

27. A puffin can drink salt water. True or False?

28. Which animal can be found in the Arctic—a tiger, a lion, or an ostrich?

29. Why does a ptarmigan have feathers on its feet?

30. Spell the word "hibernate."

31. When does a "nocturnal" animal sleep—night or day?

32. Snowy owls, like all owls, hunt at night. True or False?

33. What sea animal has a three-foot-long tooth sticking out of its lip?

34. Whales need to breathe air. True or False?

35. What word means "to sleep through the winter months?"

36. Spell the word "tundra."

37. The Amur tiger is better known by what name?

38. Why do adult musk oxen surround the babies in the herd?